The Ladybug

This book has been reviewed
for accuracy by
Walter L. Gojmerac
Professor of Entomology
University of Wisconsin—Madison.

Library of Congress Cataloging in Publication Data

Oda, Hidetomo.
The ladybug.

(Nature close-ups)
Translation of: Tentōmushi / text by Hidetomo Oda,
photographs by Nanao Kikaku.
Summary: Discusses the life cycle, behavior patterns,
and habitats of ladybugs.
1. Ladybirds—Juvenile literature. [1. Ladybugs]
I. Nanao Kikaku (Firm) II. Title. III. Series.
QL596.C6503513 1986 595.76′9 85-28199

ISBN 0-8172-2538-2 (lib. bdg.)
ISBN 0-8172-2563-3 (softcover)

This edition first published in 1986 by Raintree Publishers Inc.

1 2 3 4 5 6 7 8 9 0 90 89 88 87 86

The Ladybug

Raintree Publishers
Milwaukee

● The ladybug's underside (left) and shell (right).

From above, the only part of the ladybug one can see is its bright, spotted shell, which is actually its front pair of wings. If you turn over a ladybug, you can see its thorax, midsection, and abdomen, the segmented rear section.

Ladybugs are among the best-known of all insects. Of the almost five thousand kinds, or species, of ladybugs in the world, most are helpful to people. Ladybugs eat huge numbers of aphids, scale insects, and other harmful pests that eat garden plants and crops. Ladybugs are also called ladybirds or sun beetles.

In many countries of the world, these brightly colored beetles are thought to bring good luck. In Germany, it is believed that if a ladybug flies into a house, the family living there will become rich. During the Middle Ages, ladybugs were considered sacred. And they are still favorites of people throughout the world today.

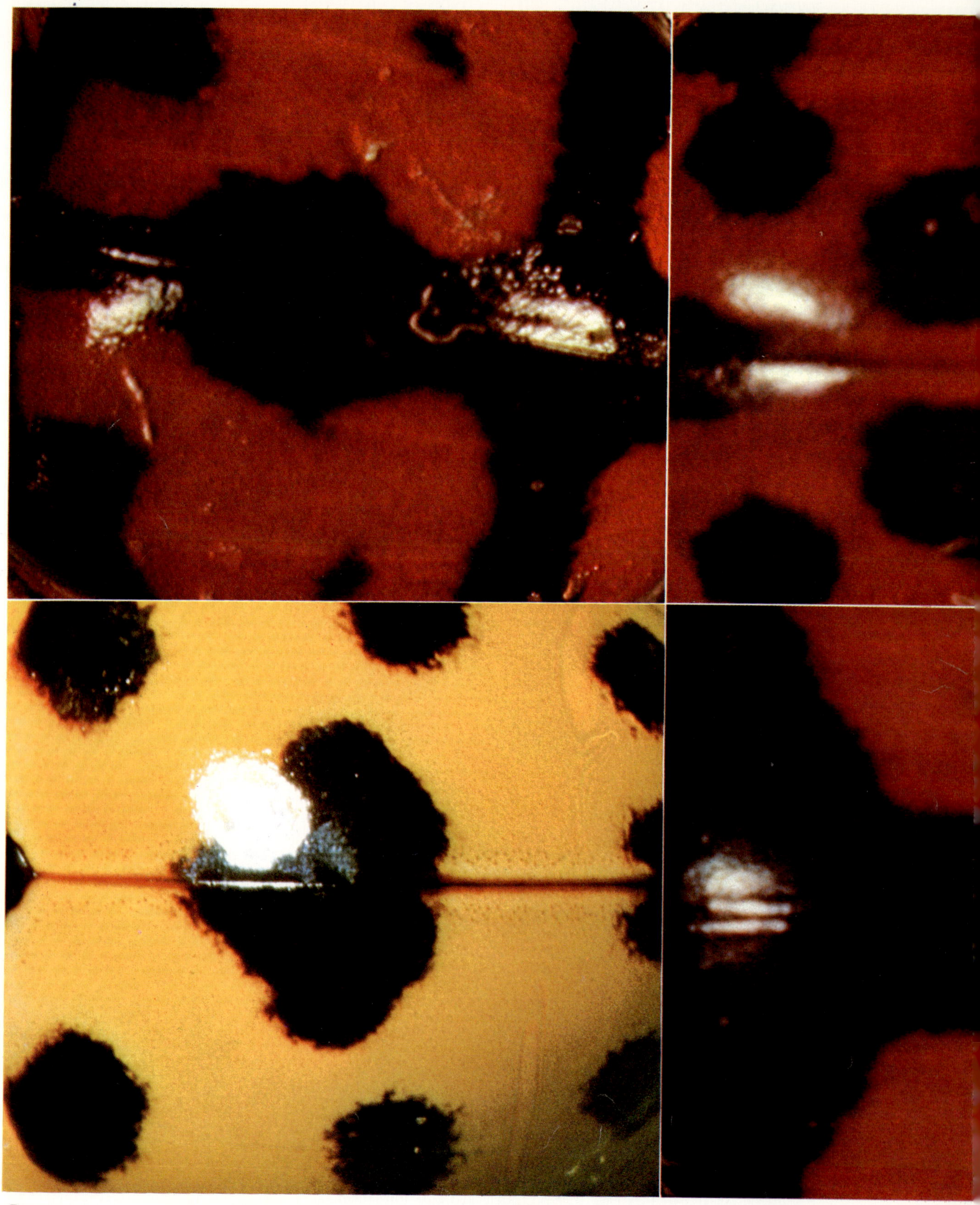

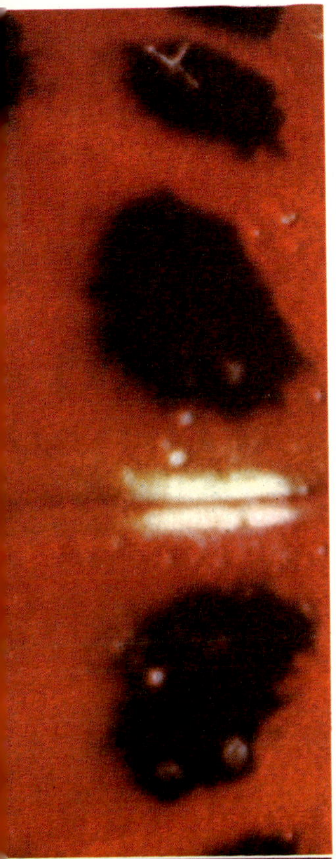

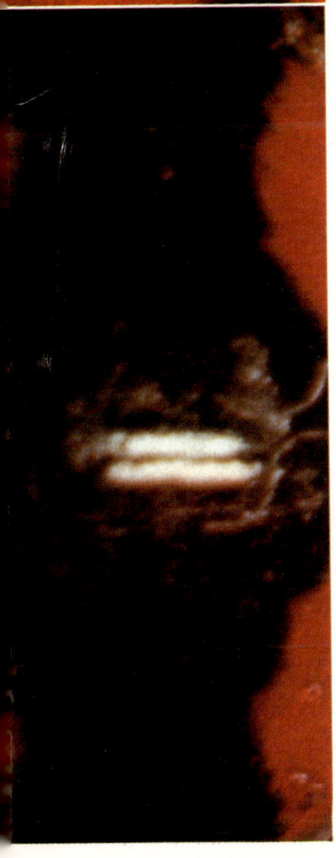

Various wing patterns.

These are some of the many wing patterns common to ladybugs. In spite of their bright colors, tiny ladybugs are easily hidden from one another in dense foliage. So they rely on their sense of smell to find other members of the same species.

Ladybugs have colorful and beautifully varied wing patterns. There are brilliant red and bright gold ladybugs with black spots. And there are shiny black ladybugs with red, orange, or gold spots. Scientists believe these differences may be the result of varying temperature and humidity in the early stages of the ladybug's development.

People instantly recognize ladybugs by their bright and beautiful wing patterns. Ladybugs, however, recognize each other by a common odor.

▶ **A ladybug on a dandelion.**

The plump ladybug walks about easily on even the most fragile of flowers. With its three pairs of short legs and jointed feet, or tarsi, it travels more efficiently on the ground than in the air.

Although ladybugs have many different wing patterns, all ladybugs have the same body structure. The head has a pair of feelers, or antennae, for touching objects and detecting odors, two compound eyes, and two sets of pincer-like jaws for seizing and chewing food.

Attached to the ladybug's thorax, or midsection, are two pairs of wings and three pairs of legs. The ladybug's jointed feet, tarsi, have tiny claws and sticky pads of hair so the beetle can climb up and down plant leaves and stems with ease.

Both the thorax and the rear part of the body, the abdomen, are protected by the elytra, the front wings, which form a hard shell. The ladybug's shell is so tough it can withstand up to eight hundred times its own weight without cracking.

▲ A ladybug crawling on plant leaves.

▲ A ladybug on a radish leaf.

Ladybugs are cold-blooded animals, which means their body temperature changes with the temperature of the air. In winter, the ladybug's body functions slow way down and it enters a period of inactivity, called hibernation. When ladybugs awaken in the spring, the first thing they do is search for food. They are very hungry because they have lived only on stored energy all winter.

Most ladybugs are carnivorous, which means they eat meat. They wander about on plant leaves and stems, hunting for insects to eat. Ladybugs can be found on a variety of plants, depending on the season. Look for them in flower gardens, or on pea, bean and radish plants.

▲ A ladybug on a stalk of wheat.

▶ A ladybug on a lotus blossom.

Ladybugs are persistent hunters, or predators, with hearty appetites. They eat scale insects, aphids, and any other small insects they can find.

The ladybug uses its sharp jaws, or mandibles, to seize its prey. It pierces its victim and, with a special tube in its mouth, shoots a liquid into the body of its prey. The liquid changes the inside of the victim's body into a soupy substance, which the ladybug ingests.

The ladybug's favorite food is a tiny, soft-bodied insect called an aphid. During the warm summer months, aphids feed on plants and multiply there in great numbers. The common ladybug eats more than a thousand aphids in its lifetime.

◀ **Ladybugs and aphids.**

Ladybugs move from plant to plant, from spring to fall, in search of aphids, their favorite food.

▶ **A black ant and aphids.**

Ants love to collect honeydew, the sweet substance secreted by aphids.

◀ **An ant collecting honeydew.**

An ant taps the aphid with its antennae and collects the sweet honeydew which it secretes.

▶ **A ladybug eating an aphid.**

The small, carnivorous ladybug moves slowly over plant stems and leaves in search of aphids. This ladybug has captured an aphid and is ingesting its body fluids.

A sure way to find ladybugs is to look for a plant where ants are hurrying up and down the stalk. Ants seem to be very fond of honeydew, a sweet substance secreted by aphids. Because of this, a special helping relationship has developed between ants and aphids.

Aphids feed by sucking sap from plants. When the ants gather around the aphids and tap or stroke them on the back with their antennae, the aphids secrete honeydew from their abdomens and the ants lick it up.

The ants, in turn, guard the aphids from predators such as ladybugs. They attack ladybugs with their sharp jaws, trying to drive them away, thus ensuring themselves a supply of honeydew.

▶ A ladybug attacked by a spider.

Spiders, birds, and praying mantises are also predators of the ladybug. Unlike many insects, ladybugs cannot sting or poison their enemies. But they do have several ways of defending themselves. Sometimes, a ladybug will draw its legs and head inside its hard shell and hide—much the way a turtle does. Or a ladybug may squirt liquid from certain joints in its legs. The liquid is yellow-orange in color and leaves a very bitter taste in the mouth of any predator that tries to attack the ladybug. When the same predator sees another brightly colored ladybug, it will remember the bitter taste and probably will not attack again.

▼ A ladybug curled up, playing dead.

▼ A ladybug secreting liquid from its leg joints.

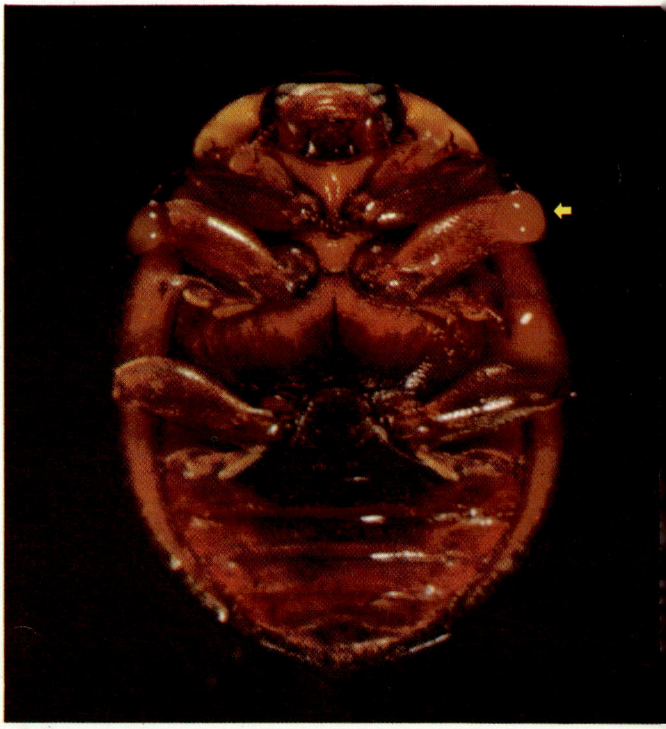

◀ **Ladybugs mating.**

Although their wing patterns differ greatly, this male and female know from each other's odor that they belong to the same species.

▶ **A ladybug laying eggs.**

In some species, the female ladybug lays eggs several times in her lifetime, up to one hundred eggs each time. Other species lay eggs about ten times in their lives but lay only about thirty eggs each time.

In order for new ladybugs to be born, adult ladybugs must mate. Ladybugs recognize other members of the same species by their odor. When a male and female ladybug of the same species meet on a plant leaf, they join their bodies and mate. The male passes sperm from his body to the female's body. The sperm unite with the eggs inside her body. The eggs are then fertilized.

About a week later, the female ladybug begins to lay her eggs. The eggs pass through a tube-like ovipositor at the end of her abdomen. She lays tiny, bright yellow eggs on a branch or leaf that will get plenty of sunlight. She chooses a plant covered with aphids so that when the eggs hatch, the developing larvae will have plenty of food to eat.

Within several days, the bright yellow eggs turn pale white and the ladybug larvae begin to emerge. These funny looking creatures with hairy bodies and long legs do not look at all like adult ladybugs. But they have enormous appetites, just as their parents do.

For their first meal, the larvae ingest the liquid from the eggs which have not yet hatched. Then, they begin to travel up

Ladybug larvae emerging from eggs.

Larvae ingesting body fluids from aphids.

and down the plant, searching for aphids.

At first, the larvae only ingest fluids from the aphids. But as they grow older, they begin to eat the bodies of their victims, as well.

Since the ladybug larva eats constantly, it outgrows its old skin. It then molts, or sheds its skin. This happens at least three times before it is ready to enter the next stage in its life cycle.

A larva shedding its old skin.

A more mature larva eating an aphid.

A larva before it becomes a pupa.

When it is fully grown, the ladybug larva stops eating, attaches itself to a branch or leaf, and remains still. It sheds its larval skin for the last time and enters the third stage in its life cycle, as a pupa. During this resting stage, mysterious changes take place. The wings, legs, and antennae of the adult ladybug are being formed.

Within five to eight days, the ladybug will emerge from the pupal skin and begin the final stage in its life cycle—as a winged adult.

A pupa.

▶ **A newly emerged ladybug.**

● **A ladybug's life cycle.**

Like many other insects, the ladybug experiences changes in its development. This process of change is called metamorphosis and has four stages: egg, larva, pupa, and adult.

When the adult ladybug first emerges from its pupal skin, it is pale yellow. But soon, both the front and hind wings will darken, and unique spot patterns will form. The species of ladybug in these pictures turns a brilliant red with shiny black spots.

After it emerges, the ladybug rests a while. Then it finds a sheltered place where it can spread its damp, wrinkled wings to dry. The front wings will soon dry and harden to form the protective wing case, called the elytra. The long, thin, transparent hind wings are kept folded and tucked inside the elytra when they are not being used in flight.

◀ **An adult ladybug drying its wings.**

The newly emerged ladybug spreads its wet, wrinkled wings to dry. Gradually they smooth out and become darker in color.

▲◀ **The ladybug's pattern grows more distinct.**

At this stage, the wings are still soft enough to dent if they are touched. As they dry, the spot pattern darkens and becomes more distinct.

Now the ladybug has wings and is ready to explore a whole new world. One of its first flights will be to a plant where aphids live and where it is likely to meet a mate.

When it wants to fly, the ladybug raises its elytra and unfolds the pair of wings hidden beneath. The hind wings beat up and down, propelling the insect forward. The elytra do not move but they act much the same way as an airplane's wings —they give the beetle "lift." But ladybugs are not very good fliers because their hind wings do not beat very rapidly.

◀ **A ladybug hunting aphids.**

Ladybugs eat as many aphids as they can in autumn before the frost comes. The aphids die in cold weather, but the ladybugs will hibernate through the winter, living on their stored energy.

▶ **A ladybug ready to fly.**

When it wants to fly, the ladybug unlocks the elytra and spreads its hind wings in readiness for flight.

A CLOSER LOOK

Let's find out

What Do Ladybugs Do in Winter?

▲ A field in winter.

Some insects spend the winter as eggs, or as pupae, but the ladybug lives through the winter as an adult. During autumn, the ladybug searches for food and eats during the day. At night, it seeks shelter from the cold near the roots of trees or under dead leaves. When winter sets in, the ladybug crawls into a deep crevice around the roots of a tree, or under fallen leaves, and hibernates. It sleeps until spring, living on the food that it stored in its body during the autumn.

Ladybugs spending the winter together.

It is possible to find thousands of ladybugs hibernating together in one place. On a fine day in late autumn, many ladybugs gather together and crawl deep into a crevice around the trunk of a tree. They bury themselves in the ground, in order to hibernate. It is still not known why so many of them hibernate in the same place. Although there are differences in color and pattern, the ladybugs pictured here all belong to the same species.

Other beetles also spend the winter as adults.

Adults of other species of hard-winged beetles also crawl into decayed wood or into the ground to spend the winter. Because they do not move in the cold, these insects need very little energy. They live on the food they stored in their bodies during the fall. In spring, the adult females lay eggs and new beetles soon emerge.

Below, an adult broad bean weevil hibernates in a broad bean (left photo); a beetle hibernates in the ground (middle photo); and a crab spider hibernates next to beetles in tree bark (right photo).

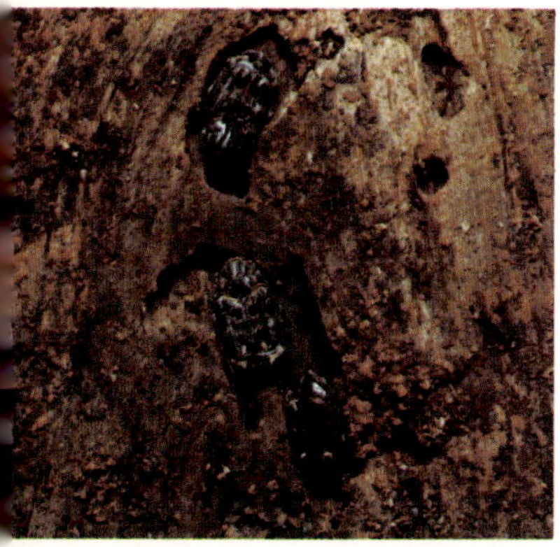

Let's find out

A CLOSER LOOK

Do the wing patterns of ladybugs differ according to the species?

▲ **Common ladybugs.**

These ladybugs with variously colored wing patterns all belong to the same common species.

There are almost five thousand species of ladybugs in the world. Scientists classify the different species according to shape, size, color, and markings. Generally, different species have different markings.

But within the common ladybug species, there are many kinds of wing markings. So, when two ladybugs with different markings mate and produce eggs, it is likely they belong to the common ladybug species.

Common ladybug markings.

Many different markings are found in the common ladybug species. Ladybugs may have two, four, twelve, or twenty spots on their wings. They may also have other numbers of spots and some have no spots at all. The shape of the spots of the ladybugs in this species may be regular or irregular. The ladybugs pictured below are all members of the common ladybug species.

● **Different kinds of ladybugs.**

▶ ***Rodolia limbata.***
This kind of ladybug eats the scale insect and is found throughout most of Japan.

▶ ***Rodolia cardinalis.***
This ladybug lives in Australia and feeds on scale insects, which damage oranges.

▶ ***Synonycha grandis.***
This species is the largest of the ladybugs found in Japan. It also eats the scale insect.

▶ ***Propylaea japonica.***
Different wing markings can be found within this species of ladybug which eats aphids.

◀ ***Aiolacaria mirabilis.***
This large ladybug, found in colder regions, eats the larvae of plant aphids.

◀ ***Epilachna admirabilis.***
This ladybug is herbivorous, which means it eats the leaves of plants.

GLOSSARY

carnivorous—a word used to describe animals that eat meat. (pp. 10, 14)

cold-blooded animal—an animal whose temperature changes with the temperature of the air. (p. 10)

compound eyes—an insect's eyes, comprised of many tiny lenses, or individual eyes. (p. 8)

elytra—a beetle's front wings, which form a protective shell over the soft hind wings. (pp. 8, 25, 26)

hibernation—a period of inactivity undergone by animals during cold weather when their body functions slow down. (pp. 10, 26, 29)

mandibles—jaws used for biting and chewing. (p. 13)

metamorphosis—a process of development during which physical changes take place. Complete metamorphosis involves four stages: egg, larva, pupa, and adult. Incomplete metamorphosis occurs in three stages: egg, nymph, and adult. (p. 23)

ovipositor—an egg-laying tube which extends from the tip of an insect's abdomen. (p. 18)

predators—animals that hunt or kill other animals for food. (pp. 13, 16)

tarsi—the jointed feet of insects. (p. 8)